UpS and DowNs

A Book About the Stock Market

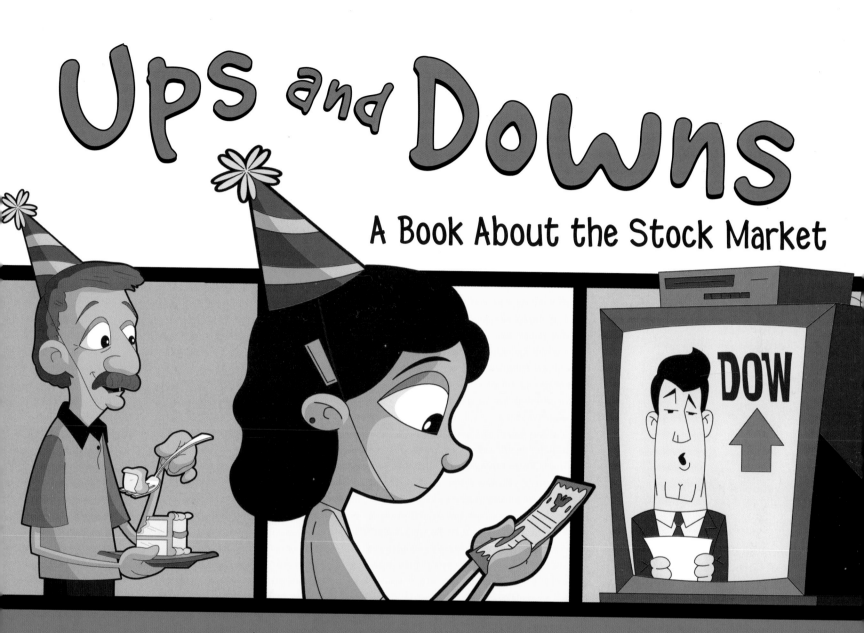

written by Nancy Loewen   *   illustrated by Brian Jensen

Thanks to our advisers for their expertise, research, and advice:

Dr. Joseph Santos
Associate Professor of Economics, Department of Economics
South Dakota State University

Susan Kesselring, M.A., Literacy Educator
Rosemount-Apple Valley-Eagan (Minnesota) School District

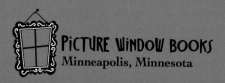

PiCTURE WiNDOW BOOKS
Minneapolis, Minnesota

Managing Editor: Catherine Neitge
Creative Director: Terri Foley
Art Director: Keith Griffin
Editors: Patricia Stockland, Christianne Jones
Designer: Nathan Gassman
Page Production: Picture Window Books
The illustrations in this book were
prepared digitally.

Picture Window Books
5115 Excelsior Boulevard
Suite 232
Minneapolis, MN 55416
877-845-8392
www.picturewindowbooks.com

**Library of Congress
Cataloging-in-Publication Data**
Loewen, Nancy, 1964-
Ups and downs : a book about the stock
market / by Nancy Loewen ; illustrated by
Brian Jensen.
p. cm. — (Money matters)
Includes bibliographical references and index.
ISBN 1-4048-0954-6 (hardcover)
1. Stock exchanges—United States—Juvenile
literature. 2. Stocks—United States—Juvenile
literature. 3. Investments—United States—
Juvenile literature. I. Jensen, Brian, ill. II. Title.
III. Money matters (Minneapolis, Minn.)

HG4572.L57 2005
332.64'273—dc22   2004019743

Shannon tore off the paper and opened her final present. Inside was some sort of certificate.

"It's a single share of Taco Bill stock!" Uncle Joe said. "Congratulations, Shannon, you're a shareholder now!"

"Oh," said Shannon. "Uh, thanks, Uncle Joe."

3

"Let me explain," said Uncle Joe. "Lots of big companies sell units of ownership to the public. That's what a share of stock is—it means you actually own a small piece of the company."

Stocks can also be called securities, or equities. Companies sell stock and use the money to make the company grow.

5

"Do I just put this certificate on the wall?" Shannon asked.

"You can," Uncle Joe said. "But what's really fun is that you can keep track of its value on the stock market."

The United States has three main stock exchanges. The biggest one is the New York Stock Exchange.

"What does that mean?" Shannon asked.

"The value of stocks is always changing," Uncle Joe explained. "The price just depends on how much people think it's worth. People buy and sell stocks in an organization called a stock exchange."

7

Uncle Joe got a newspaper and opened it to the business section. The heading said NYSE, for New York Stock Exchange. Shannon saw rows and rows of tiny numbers and letters.

"TACB is the symbol of Taco Bill," Uncle Joe said. "And here, this number is the price. I bought the stock four days ago for $25.12. Now it's up to $25.75. You've already made 63 cents."

"Cool," said Shannon.

Stock prices vary a lot, depending on the company. A single share can be less than a dollar—or hundreds of dollars.

9

The next day, Shannon's mother showed her how to track her investment online.

"People are always buying and selling shares of stock on Wall Street in New York," Mom explained. "But not just anyone can walk in and place an order. Only brokers can do that. They have special training and are licensed. They place orders for their clients."

"And the price depends on how many people want the stock and how much they're willing to pay for it," Shannon said.

"You've got it," said Mom.

When people buy stock, they pay a commission, or fee, to the broker.

11

Shannon checked her stock a lot. It was going up a little bit every day. But one day Shannon checked her stock and discovered it was down 50 cents.

Shannon called Uncle Joe.

"What's happening?" she asked.

"Taco Bill hasn't been making as much money as people expected," he said. "And that makes people value their stock less. Plus, the entire market has been down lately, which affects your stock."

Stock Market Report

Investing in the stock market involves risk. While stocks can increase greatly in value, they might also become worthless.

13

"What if I keep losing money?" Shannon asked.

"Well, you could sell your stock," said Uncle Joe. "Right now you'd get less than it was worth when you got it. But that way you'd be sure to get something out of it."

"Let's sell!" said Shannon.

"Let's think about this," said Uncle Joe. "Taco Bill is a good company. If you ride out the tough times, the stock price is likely to go up again."

"Oh," said Shannon. "I'll keep it then."

The stock market is best for long-term investing (more than five years). Historically, stocks have made more money than other kinds of investments.

Over the next few weeks, Shannon's stock slowly regained its value. And Shannon learned even more about the stock market. She discovered that people don't always have to buy individual stocks. They can buy shares of mutual funds, which hold stock in lots of different companies.

Mutual funds collect money from thousands, even millions, of investors. The risk is spread out among many companies, so holding shares of a mutual fund can be a safer way to invest.

One evening on the news, a business reporter said that the Dow was up.

"Hey!" said Shannon. "I know what that means! It's the Dow Jones Industrial Average. It's this group of 30 companies that are supposed to be like the whole market. The Dow is a number that gives people an idea of what the market is doing."

"I'm so impressed," said Mom. "Uncle Joe's birthday gift has really paid off!"

In addition to the Dow, other market indicators include the NASDAQ and the S & P (Standard & Poor's) 500.

In December, Shannon's grandpa sent her some money for Christmas. She knew just what to do with it. She called Uncle Joe right away.

"I want to use my Christmas money to buy some shares of a mutual fund," she said. "Can you help me set it up?"

"Great idea!" said Uncle Joe. "I'd be happy to help you."

Learn to Read a Stock Listing

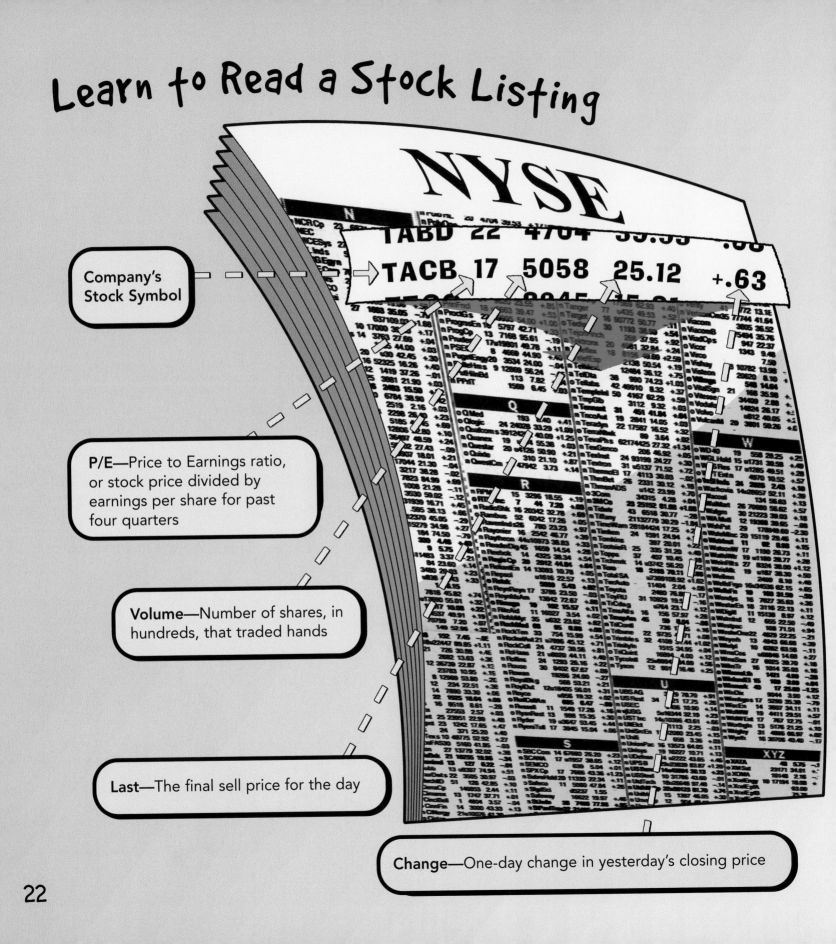

Company's Stock Symbol

P/E—Price to Earnings ratio, or stock price divided by earnings per share for past four quarters

Volume—Number of shares, in hundreds, that traded hands

Last—The final sell price for the day

Change—One-day change in yesterday's closing price

Fun Facts

- When most stock prices are going up over a period of months, it's called a bull market. When most stock prices are going down, it's called a bear market. A crash is when prices go down very quickly.

- The worst U.S. stock market crash in history took place in 1929. It led to the Great Depression, a time when many people were out of work.

- More than half of all households in the United States have money invested in the stock market.

- You must be at least 18 years old to invest in the stock market. However, parents or guardians can open custodial accounts for younger investors.

Glossary

certificate—a paper that gives proof of something

clients—people who pay for professional services

custodial—when an adult has authority to make decisions for a child

investment—money that is given to a business in the hope of getting more money back in the future

licensed—having permission from the government to do a certain job

profits—money that a business makes after expenses have been subtracted

risk—the chance of losing money

TO LEARN MORE

At the Library

Barbash, Fred. *Investing Your Money*. Philadelphia: Chelsea House, 2001.

Giesecke, Ernestine. *Playing the Market: Stocks and Bonds*. Chicago: Heinemann Library, 2003.

Young, Robin R. *The Stock Market*. Minneapolis: Lerner, 1991.

On the Web

FactHound offers a safe, fun way to find Web sites related to this book. All of the sites on FactHound have been researched by our staff. *www.facthound.com*

1. Visit the FactHound home page.

2. Enter a search word related to this book, or type in this special code: 1404809546

3. Click on the FETCH IT button.

Your trusty FactHound will fetch the best sites for you!

INDEX

Look for all of the books in this series:

- Cash, Credit Cards, or Checks: A Book About Payment Methods

- Lemons and Lemonade: A Book About Supply and Demand

- Save, Spend, or Donate? A Book About Managing Money

- Ups and Downs: A Book About the Stock Market